Gordon Winter

GORDON WINTER

Kenneth T. Williams

Gordon Winter
first published 2012 by
Scirocco Drama
An imprint of J. Gordon Shillingford Publishing Inc.

Reprinted 2018, 2020

Scirocco Drama Editor: Glenda MacFarlane
Cover design by Terry Gallagher/Doowah Design Inc.
Author photo by Stefen Winchester
Printed and bound in Canada on 100% post-consumer recycled paper.

We acknowledge the financial support of the Manitoba Arts Council and The Canada Council for the Arts for our publishing program.

Production inquiries should be addressed to:
Charles Northcote, Core Literary Inc.
140 Wolfrey Avenue
Toronto, ON M4K 1L3
416-466-4929
charlesnorthcote@rogers.com

Library and Archives Canada Cataloguing in Publication

Williams, Kenneth T., 1965-
Gordon Winter / Kenneth T. Williams

A play.
ISBN 978-1-897289-72-3

I. Title.

PS8645.I4525G67 2012 C812'.6 C2012-901276-9

J. Gordon Shillingford Publishing
P.O. Box 86, RPO Corydon Avenue, Winnipeg, MB Canada R3M 3S3

For Gordon Tootoosis

Scene

The action should be fluid, with a minimal set and multipurpose props. The cast should be multicultural. The play can be done with six actors. Gordon Winter, in all his incarnations, is played by one actor.

Time

Northern woods of Saskatchewan 1944, bush plane crash site 1971, and Saskatoon in the present.

Notes on Dialogue

There are dashes and brackets during some speeches. The "--" represent the speech being interrupted by the following speaker. The words between the [ ] represent what the character would have said if they weren't interrupted.

Characters

GORDON WINTER:	As he is now, as an RCMP officer in the 1970s and as a 6-year-old. These are all played by the same actor.
REPORTERS:	The barking dogs of the media.
CYNTHIA HENHAWK:	Mohawk, young, recently passed the bar in Saskatchewan, and Winter's court-appointed lawyer. She doesn't "look" Aboriginal.
SHALINI O'MALLEY:	South Asian-Canadian, Cynthia's best friend and roommate, she works with an agency that helps recent immigrants adjust to life in Canada.
DAVID, ALEXANDRA & FOSTER:	Co-workers and friends of Shalini.
ISIAH CHARLES:	85, Cree, prisoner being escorted by bush plane from Pelican Narrows to Prince Albert.
DOUG NAPIER:	Bush pilot.
FRANK TKACHUK:	Crown prosecutor.
HON. BETTY FRIEDMAN:	Judge.
JASMINE RAIN:	Radio talk show host.
HON. CARL SMITH:	Judge.

STENOGRAPHER:	Court reporter, waitress.
ANTON KRUPINSKI:	Afrika Korps officer, a POW in Canada.
MUSHOM:	Gordon's grandfather, a veteran of World War 1.
GRANT:	An RCMP constable.
CALLERS:	The radio listeners who call in to Jasmine's show.
PROTESTOR:	Anti-Israel, pro-Palestinian protestor.
QUEEN ELIZABETH II:	Her majesty, the Queen.
PRINCIPAL McADAMS:	Residential school principal.
DANIEL:	6, a child at the residential school.
CHILDREN:	Young children at the residential school.

Production History

Gordon Winter had its world premiere at Persephone Theatre, in Saskatoon, Saskatchewan on October 13, 2010, with the following cast and crew:

Gordon Winter .... Gordon Tootoosis

Cynthia Henhawk, Reporter, Children .... Jamie Lee Shebelski

Doug Napier, Frank Tkackuk, David, Const. Grant, Principal McAdams, Reporter, Caller .... Joshua Beaudry

Isiah Charles, Anton Krupinski, Foster, Judge Carl Smith, Reporter, Stenographer .... Robert Benz

Mushom, Jasmine Rain, Judge Betty Friedman, Alexandra, Queen Elizabeth II, Children, Reporter, Stenographer .... Kim Harvey

Shalini O'Malley, Reporter, Protestor, Daniel .... Keisha Haines

Directed by Del Surjik

Assistant Director: Rob Roy

Set, Lighting and Sound Design by Jim Guedo

Costume Design by Carla Orosz

Stage Manager: Jennifer Rathie-Wright

Playwright's Notes

Gordon Tootoosis seemed indestructable. There was a permanence to him, like he was the stone of a mountain or a towering cedar. You could rely on him. He would always be there, smiling, joking but steady and knowledgeable. His presence meant everything was going to be all right. Yet, despite his age, he never lost the spark of youth. When he smiled at you, you never knew what impish fun he was about to unleash.

It didn't matter how long you knew him, five minutes or five decades, he made you feel like you were the most important person in the world. That was his gift. He may have been a movie star but he never acted like it. Gordon's attachment to the play garnered a lot of media attention but he always insisted that the spotlight shine on the other actors or myself. The cast and crew of *Gordon Winter* immediately fell for him.

When we heard he had died of pneumonia, we were gutted. The mountain had fallen. The stone had shattered. But his presence can still be felt in the hours and hours of television and film reels and in many indelable memories he created when he walked on the stage.

Thank you Gordon for your dedication and love of theatre. You will always be remembered.

Kenneth T. Williams

Kenneth T. Williams is a Cree playwright, photographer and journalist from the George Gordon First Nation. His plays *Café Daughter, Gordon Winter, Thunderstick, Bannock Republic, Suicide Notes* and *Three Little Birds* have been professionally produced across Canada. *Thunderstick* has recently been optioned as a feature film project. *Thunderstick* and *Bannock Republic* were published by Scirocco Drama, with *Suicide Notes* published in the anthology, *Three On the Boards,* by Signature Editions. He blogs about his playwriting adventures on his website feralplaywright.ca. He also teaches playwriting at the University of Saskatchewan. As well as writing plays, Kenneth has edited three series for television. He is the first Aboriginal writer to earn an M.F.A. in playwriting from the University of Alberta. He currently resides in Saskatoon.

Act I

Scene 1

We're in a bar. On a TV, GORDON WINTER is at a lectern in an auditorium. GORDON WINTER enters and glares at the audience.

GORDON: I want to thank the Elders and veterans for asking me to speak this morning.

A cell phone rings.

Turn off your goddamn cell phones and listen up. You chiefs, you young chiefs, are letting the federal government trample our treaty rights…again! I've been waiting for one of you to stand up and show me that you've got the balls to tell the government to back off. But no. You don't want to threaten your precious funding agreements. God forbid you don't get to fly to Vegas on another "fact-finding" mission on gambling. You're in the pockets of the federal government and you're getting comfortable in there. You're asleep and the feds know it. Wan-ska! Wake up! The feds keep saying they're honouring our treaty rights. They say signing this form is just a technicality. That they need this information to "protect" us. But if we don't fill out these forms, we don't get the medicine we need, that we're promised under treaty. This doesn't protect us. It takes our private information and shares it with anyone who wants to look at it. Our people need medicine, they don't need paperwork! It's not protection, it's blackmail! You chiefs are either too gutless or too stupid to stop this nonsense. Are you all so out of touch with the treaties that you need workshops to explain how you're getting screwed by the feds? When Trudeau dropped the White Paper on us we didn't need any workshops to stop that nonsense. And when he wanted to repatriate the constitution did you think he invited us to the table to discuss our place in it? We banged the goddamn door down and said, you can't negotiate this without us. We knew we were right because we knew the treaties. The treaties that the government of Canada now finds so inconvenient. Well it's time to be inconvenient again, people. Show me what kind of balls you have. Do you need a per diem cheque before you'll tell the government to fuck off? I want to see you, all of you, take out those cheques. Right now. Rip them up. Right now, goddamn it! *(Pause.)* I didn't think so. Gutless. What are your grandchildren going to think of you when they find out you gave away their rights for a new truck? I didn't fight for my grandchildren's rights so you could piss them away. What kind of country are we leaving them when Pakis, faggots and other trash that wash up have more rights than our children! Hitler had the good sense to wipe away such filth.

The REPORTERS scrum him, barking when they're not asking him a question, talking over him.

GORDON: Is this how you're going to get the government to listen? "Please, Mr. Health Minister, don't make us sign these pieces of paper." You don't ask them to bend. You make them bend! You make them bend because your grandmother will have to fill out a form that will be written in English and French but not in Cree, or Saulteaux, or Dene. A form that will stop your grandmother from getting that bottle of oxygen that she needs. A form that will stop a young mother from getting the prescription for her children. This form doesn't solve our problems.

REPORTERS: *(Barking, chaotic, repeating, drowning out GORDON.)* What did you mean when you said "Hitler?" Are you anti-immigrant? This country was built by immigrants, why would you say they're trash? How can you hate Pakis when they look just like you? Doesn't your culture celebrate two-spirited people?

GORDON: Our people are sick. They need medicine. That medicine is our right!

Scene 2

GORDON's office. He's packing it up. Several boxes lie around, stuff piled up everywhere. CYNTHIA HENHAWK enters.

CYNTHIA: Dr. Winter, I'm Cynthia Henhawk and I'm— [your lawyer.]

GORDON: Henhawk? That's one of them Iroquois names, right?

CYNTHIA: Haudenasaunee.

GORDON: Hoh-duh-nah-SHO-nee.

CYNTHIA: We've got a lot to discuss.

GORDON: We got nothing to discuss. I didn't hire you. I don't need you. Fuck off.

CYNTHIA: You got me. Judge Friedman said so and there's nothing you or I can do about that.

GORDON: Hoh-duh-nah-SHO-nee. Must be nice, looking like a moniyaw and getting all those rights I fought for.

CYNTHIA: That's not— [helpful.]

GORDON: What's a Haudenasaunee lawyer doing in

Saskatchewan? Not enough drunk drivers on Six Nations?

CYNTHIA: I graduated here.

GORDON: I see. Another fine product of the First Peoples Law Program.

CYNTHIA: Yes.

GORDON: Have they erased my name from that plaque yet?

CYNTHIA: No, sir, they haven't.

GORDON: Everyone else seems pretty quick to get rid of me. Rats, all of them. Goddamn rats. Even the chiefs are running scared.

GORDON picks up a framed photo from the box and hands it to CYNTHIA.

That's the Queen pinning the medal of bravery onto my chest when she visited in 1973. You think she's sending a letter to have the RCMP take that away from me as well?

He snaps the photo out from CYNTHIA's hand and slams it into the garbage.

Listen to me, Miss Haudenasaunee-lawyer and listen good. I am not making a deal with the government. They can go to hell if they think I'm pleading guilty.

CYNTHIA: It's a good deal.

GORDON: They can shove it up their ass!

CYNTHIA: Just apologize and they'll recommend a conditional discharge.

GORDON: Apologize! For defending the rights of my grandchildren!

CYNTHIA: Dr. Winter, please— [we need to…]

GORDON: Dirty Injun Dirty Injun Dirty Injun! That's what those fucking fresh off the boat Paki kids were chanting at my grandson. My eight-year-old grandson. In the schoolyard. Right in front of his teachers who stood by and said nothing. They told his mom that they could put those kids in some sensitivity bullshit class but they couldn't punish them because they were afraid of offending those poor Pakis'— [feelings.]

CYNTHIA: Stop calling them Pakis!

GORDON: Get out.

CYNTHIA: I wish I could.

GORDON: Get the hell out!

CYNTHIA: I can't!

GORDON: You're fired.

CYNTHIA: Only the judge can do that.

GORDON: Fuck the judge. I'll defend myself.

CYNTHIA: You're not a lawyer, you stubborn son-of-a-bitch. You are stuck with me.

GORDON: Dirty Injun Dirty Injun. Anyone ever call you that, Miss Henhawk? Huh? Didn't think so. You walk down the street and you know what people think? "Oooh, there's a successful young woman. Nice clothes. Shiny shoes. Hair done up." You fit in. You don't make white people uncomfortable. You don't challenge them. You play by their rules. You are invisible. Because you're a good Indian.

CYNTHIA: You know what? I'll do this without your help. Here's my card.

She tosses some cards into the box GORDON is

packing. Before she leaves, she grabs the broken frame and peels the photo out from within.

I'll be in touch.

She leaves. End of Scene 2.

Scene 3

The bar. DAVID, ALEXANDRA and FOSTER are SHALINI's friends and the they're very drunk. CYNTHIA enters, still carrying her briefcase, and plops herself down on the couch. The other three are oblivious to her. SHALINI enters with a drink which she gives to CYNTHIA.

SHALINI: You look terrible.

CYNTHIA: Had a shitty day.

DAVID: Why did Hitler go to Alcoholics Anonymous?

ALEXANDRA: David, no.

FOSTER: Hitler didn't drink.

DAVID: *(Mocking a deaf person.)* It'th a thoke, Fothter. Not a hithtory lethon.

ALEXANDRA: Hitler didn't drink?

FOSTER: Nope. Didn't smoke or eat meat either.

ALEXANDRA: He was a vegetarian!

FOSTER: Yep. He was totally into clean living.

DAVID: OK, OK, for the sake of the joke, let's say Hitler drank. A lot. OK? He goes totally Indian with the rye. Sorry, I meant "Firsht Nayshuns, eh."

They laugh.

CYTNHIA: Your friends are hiii-larious.

SHALINI: Oh, lighten up, Cynth. They're just burning off steam. It was one of those weeks at the centre.

CYNTHIA: If I said, "Pakis, faggots and trash? Jus' jokes. L-O-L." That make you feel better?

SHALINI: But it wasn't "jus jokes" with Winter. He meant what he said.

CYNTHIA: I don't have a way out of this.

She opens her briefcase and pulls out WINTER's photo.

FOSTER: Dude, your accent totally sucks. Like this. *(Drunk Indian stereotype.)* "Yer pah-shah-nit. Da likker stoor. Yer pah-shah-nit."

They laugh.

DAVID: Jesus, man, get a spit-guard.

ALEXANDRA: *(Giggling.)* You sound exactly like one of my clients. God. I shouldn't laugh.

DAVID: The one with her front teeth missing?

ALEXANDRA: Yep. She says it's made her the most popular hooker by the hospital.

FOSTER: Why?

ALEXANDRA & DAVID: You don't know!

FOSTER: No, I don't.

DAVID mimes giving head to a beer bottle. Now FOSTER gets it.

ALEXANDRA: Nice technique, David. Did you learn that at the Aboriginal career fair?

DAVID
& FOSTER: Whooooah!

CYNTHIA: *(To Alexandra.)* Hey, bitch! Would you say that to her face? Do you know why she's out there, working the streets? You work with these women, have some respect.

ALEXANDRA: Sorry.

DAVID: *(To SHALINI.)* Friend of yours?

SHALINI: *(To DAVID.)* Yes, my "Mohawk" roommate. Remember, I told you she was coming. *(To CYNTHIA.)* They didn't mean anything by it. *(To her friends.)* Did you guys?

DAVID: Yeah, sorry.

FOSTER: We didn't know…that you were Native—

ALEXANDRA: Mohawk—

FOSTER: Mohawk! It's hard to tell.

CYNTHIA: What's hard to tell?

FOSTER: You kinda don't look like the Indians—the Natives—the First Nations we have around here. In Saskatoon. Here. That we see lots of. They're browner or something. Not too many Mohawks. Maybe it's the hair. Or the blue eyes. Shalini didn't mention you were so cute.

ALEXANDRA: *(To FOSTER.)* Just say sorry and shut the fuck up.

FOSTER: Sorry.

SHALINI pulls CYNTHIA away.

CYNTHIA: Imagine if your clients heard the things they say. Or a reporter. Wouldn't look good for the centre, would it?

SHALINI: I would love for a reporter to come down to the centre and see what we have to deal with every day. But the people we take care of aren't "newsworthy" enough. Our clients won't or can't take care of themselves. It gets pretty frustrating. So if we didn't laugh about it…

ALEXANDRA: *(To FOSTER.)* Oh hey, I finally saw *Schindler's List*, asshole. It's not even remotely funny.

FOSTER: I said watch *Life is Beautiful*. That's the funny one about the Holocaust.

DAVID: There's a comedy about the Holocaust?

FOSTER: The jokes just write themselves.

ALEXANDRA: You can't make jokes about the Holocaust.

DAVID: Ah, a challenge. Let's see… How did they get so many Jews to Auschwitz?

No one answers.

Free train rides.

They all groan.

What? Too soon?

ALEXANDRA: David, please. I just saw *Schindler's List*. They treated them worse than animals.

FOSTER: Maybe if they were treated like animals, they could've been saved by those ethical animal nutjobs.

ALEXANDRA: Like Hitler!

DAVID: Exactly! If they'd acted like cows then a bunch of veg-head protesters would've blocked the trains chanting "I'd rather go naked than kill Jews! I'd rather go naked than kill Jews."

FOSTER: Mooing Jews?

FOSTER & DAVID: *(Imitating mooing cows.)* Jooooooze. Jooooze. Jooooooooooze. Jooze!

CYNTHIA: You guys are sick!

FOSTER: What? You're Jewish too?

SHALINI pulls her away.

SHALINI: Just keep it down guys. You're not the only ones in the bar.

FOSTER, ALEXANDRA and DAVID fade. SHALINI takes the photo.

Really? That's the Queen giving him a medal?

CYNTHIA: If it wasn't for Gordon Winter, I wouldn't have gone to law school. He inspired me.

SHALINI: Before you knew he was a bigot.

CYNTHIA: It doesn't change what he did. He made sure the rights of First Nations people were protected in the constitution. He started the program here that is the world centre for Indigenous laws and traditions and treaties.

SHALINI: You sound like you're trying to talk yourself into it.

CYNTHIA: I'm doing this because the judge ordered me to.

SHALINI: So why did he get a medal?

Scene 4

REPORTERS: *(Howling, talking over each other.)* A small plane has crashed in the North. The chartered plane was carrying two passengers. No signal beacon. Bad weather is hampering any search efforts. Last seen taking off from Pelican Narrows. RCMP Constable, Gordon Winter, was on a prisoner escort. Single engine plane from Prince Albert. Blizzard expected to last for days. Three people on board.

We see DOUG, the pilot, trapped in the wreckage. GORDON staggers towards him and tries to free him.

DOUG: Don't let me die. Please God, don't let me die here.

ISIAH CHARLES, in handcuffs, staggers towards the other two.

ISIAH: I told you, we should've stayed in Pelican.

GORDON: Shut up.

ISIAH: But no one wants to listen to the crazy, old Indian. What does he know?

GORDON tries lifting DOUG out of the wreck. He screams. GORDON softly lowers him.

Leave him. He's a goner.

GORDON: I told you to shut up.

ISIAH: I know this land. The two of us, we can make it out. I know how.

DOUG: I speak Cree, you old fuck! I know what you're saying.

GORDON: We're not leaving him.

ISIAH: He'll slow us down and kill us. It's the only way the white man knows how to say "thank you."

GORDON pulls out his keys and unlocks ISIAH's handcuffs.

GORDON: Get lost or get help.

GORDON goes back to helping DOUG. He can't untangle him.

ISIAH: Fuck. I'll go make a shelter.

ISIAH exits.

GORDON: I'm sorry, Doug, but this is going to hurt like hell.

DOUG: Beats freezing to death.

GORDON: Think of Nadia and the boys.

GORDON pulls at DOUG to untangle him. Immediately, DOUG screams. He begs GORDON to stop over and over but GORDON just keeps pulling and untangling. GORDON finally has DOUG untangled and out of the plane, lying on the ground.

DOUG: I can't do this. Please, no more.

GORDON: Your leg is bad.

He makes a tourniquet with DOUG's belt and applies it to DOUG's left leg.

DOUG: Fuck Gordon! No fucking more! Please, I beg you. No more.

ISIAH returns carrying GORDON's holster.

ISIAH: I found your gun, Red Coat.

GORDON: Give it here.

ISIAH: We could put him out of his misery.

GORDON: Give me the gun.

ISIAH: Hey, white man, you want the pain to go away? It'll be over in a second.

ISIAH quickly draws the gun from the holster. GORDON stands between ISIAH and DOUG.

Stand aside, Red Coat.

Pause. GORDON calmly pulls the gun from ISIAH's hand.

GORDON: Go make that shelter.

GORDON pushes ISIAH away who leaves to make the shelter.

DOUG: Thank you.

GORDON: Tell me that when we're out of this. *(Sighs, rubs his side.)* I think I cracked some ribs.

Scene 5

JUDGE BETTY FRIEDMAN's chambers. FRANK TKACHUK is pacing. CYNTHIA enters. FRANK marches towards CYNTHIA ready with a quick handshake. GORDON sits in his empty office. SHALINI is in their apartment, sipping cocktails.

FRANK: Frank, Frank Tkachuk. Welcome to the club.

CYNTHIA: Thanks.

FRANK: Cynthia Henhawk is it? Glad you're on board, Henhawk. Maybe we can get this all settled. Finally. I mean, Betty's going nuts. And she's not a judge that—I mean—she's really easy going. When I drew her for this case, I thought, fuck, so much for my slam dunk. *(Laughs.)* Just kidding. No slam dunks when justice is on the line. Sometimes I think, for me anyways, it's the toughest cases that turn out to be the most satisfying. You've read the plea conditions, right?

CYNTHIA: Yes.

FRANK: It's a good offer.

CYNTHIA: It is.

FRANK: Henhawk? That's cool. What is that?

CYNTHIA: It's a fairly common name from— [Six Nations.]

FRANK: No. I mean what kind of hawk is that. I've never heard of it.

CYNTHIA: It's a small hawk.

FRANK: That eats hens.

CYNTHIA: I guess so.

FRANK: 'Cause you know, it kind of reminds me of Bugs Bunny. The one who keeps saying "I'm not a chicken, I'm a chicken hawk. And you're a loud mouth schnook!" Remember that little guy? Man he was funny. A real pain in Foghorn's ass, if you know what I mean.

CYNTHIA: No, I'm not sure— [what you mean.]

FRANK: I guess you're kind of young for that. Always cracked me up. Funny stuff. Bugs. Daffy too. Ah, the judge.

BETTY FRIEDMAN and the STENOGRAPHER enter. CYNTHIA and FRANK stand, and remain standing until BETTY sits down. The STENOGRAPHER sets up his gear next to the Judge. He records the following.

BETTY: Sorry to keep you waiting.

FRANK: No problemo, judge. I was just getting to know my new friend here. Finally we can move things along.

BETTY: Don't get ahead of yourself, Mr. Tkachuk.

FRANK: Of course, Judge, of course.

BETTY: It's your party, Miss Henhawk. What do you have for us?

CYNTHIA: I can't faithfully represent Dr. Winter, your honour. He wants nothing to do with me.

BETTY: I knew it would be difficult, Miss Henhawk. But here we are.

FRANK: What did he say to the proposal?

GORDON: The Crown can shove it up their ass!

Pause.

CYNTHIA: Ahhhhm… No deal.

FRANK: That stupid, old fool!

BETTY: Mr. Tkachuk, please.

FRANK: My apologies, Judge, Henhawk.

BETTY: Trial date, then?

CYNTHIA: I can't prepare for a trial if my so-called client won't speak to me.

BETTY: Do the best you can, Miss Henhawk. If he insists on representing himself, there's nothing we can do about it. But I have no confidence he can mount a proper defense. I want you in court with Dr. Winter so he doesn't make it worse for himself. You're stuck with him. Like we are.

SHALINI: You told me you were trying to get off this case.

CYNTHIA: We're not stuck if you dismiss the case, judge.

FRANK: Hold on a minute— [we're not about…]

BETTY: Mr. Tkachuk.

FRANK: Dr. Winter should've argued that point at prelim.

CYNTHIA: He didn't understand the process.

FRANK: That's his problem for firing his lawyers.

CYNTHIA: This case doesn't serve justice, your honour. What he said was unfortunate and hurtful but what he said didn't incite hatred or lead to a breach of the peace.

SHALINI: What he said was criminal. Not just unfortunate or hurtful!

FRANK: Section 319 says "likely lead to a breach of the peace." Just because it hasn't happened yet or won't happen in the future is no defense. The criminal code says it was a "willful promotion of hate against an identifiable group."

CYNTHIA: Your honour, it's been nearly a year since he made those statements and what has been the effect? No synagogues vandalized. No gay bashing incidents. No random attacks on immigrants. He hasn't repeated his statements but we keep reading them almost every other week in newspapers.

GORDON
& EVERYONE ELSE
ECHOING: What kind of country are we leaving them when Pakis, faggots and other trash that wash up have more rights than our children! Hitler had the good sense to wipe away such filth.

SHALINI: *(To GORDON.)* You fucker!

FRANK: OK, so we're skipping right to trial now judge?

BETTY: He's right, Miss Henhawk. I can't dismiss this case. We're way past that point.

CYNTHIA: Well, your honour, I wonder how seriously the Crown is taking this case when they've offered to plead this out to a conditional discharge.

BETTY: Is that true, Mr. Tkachuk?

FRANK: If he pleads guilty, yes. And gives a contrite and sincere apology with community service.

SHALINI: Fuck! "I'm sorry for advocating genocide. Please forgive me."

FRANK: But if we go to trial that's not on the table anymore.

CYNTHIA: It sounds like the Crown is looking for an easy way out. Considering all the political pressure they were under to lay charges.

FRANK: There was no pressure.

BETTY: Oh, come on, Mr. Tkachuk. Even you read the newspapers.

FRANK: OK, there was a little pressure.

CYNTHIA: If the Crown drops the charges— [then justice is…]

FRANK: The Crown is not dropping the charges. It's not in the interest of…justice.

SHALINI: An apology is not justice.

BETTY: Miss Henhawk, if Dr. Winter doesn't accept the Crown's proposal then we must discuss a trial date.

CYNTHIA: There's just one more thing, your honour. I'm asking you to remove yourself.

FRANK: On what grounds?

BETTY: Stop trying to do my job, Mr. Tkachuk.

FRANK: Sorry, Judge.

BETTY: Miss Henhawk?

CYNTHIA: You're on the board of Temple Beth Israel.

FRANK: Because she's Jewish?

CYNTHIA: Because several members of that board are also on the organizing committee of the Saskatchewan Holocaust Memorial Society. Can you honestly say, your honour, that you will be totally above their influence?

FRANK: That's ridiculous, Judge, this case has been languishing long enough.

BETTY: You're right. And it will have to find a new judge. I know I picked the right person, Miss Henhawk. I am removing myself from this case.

She nods to the STENOGRAPHER who stops recording.

And, between us and these four walls, thank you for getting me out of this mess. Good luck, to you both.

FRANK: You wouldn't happen to know how to get me out of this, do you?

CYNTHIA: Sorry.

FRANK: All right. O'Shea's anyone? First round's on me.

BETTY: I'm in. Cynthia?

SHALINI and CYNTHIA are now in their apartment.

SHALINI: Cynthia? Cynthia. Those kids Winter called Pakis. They're Sri Lankan. Refugees. From the war.

GORDON: Filth.

SHALINI: They would've been killed if they stayed there.

GORDON: Dirty Injun Dirty Injun Dirty Injun!

CYNTHIA: I won't defend what he said. But I will defend him from this criminal charge.

Scene 6

Radio call in show with JASMINE RAIN.

JASMINE: Good afternoon, Neechees. The government is dead set on prosecuting Gordon Winter for spewing hate against homosexuals, immigrants and Jews. Tell us what you think. The lines are open. Caller one, what's your mind?

CALLER 1: He said nothing about Jews. But you mention Hitler and they get all crazy. What's up with that?

JASMINE: What's up with that! Geeeeeze, it's not like they don't have a reason. Sheesh, come on people, get an education. OK, caller two, you're on.

CALLER 2: Here's an educacion—what about our holocaust? The Jews start screaming "holocaust holocaust" when they only lost six million. We lost like 200 maybe 300 million. They deny our holocaust. Isn't that like a hate crime too?

JASMINE: Whoa. Must mean this baby boom business is nothing new to us. Looks like we're taking back this country, one baby at a time. Just jokes, my wap-skwoo-wee-yas friends. OK, caller, you're live.

CALLER 3: We should boycott Israel. Stop the Palestinian genocide!

JASMINE: What has that got to do with anything? Come on, people, stay on topic. What about the trial itself and what Winter said?

CALLER 4: I'm not defending what Chief Winter said.

JASMINE: I don't think anyone is.

CALLER 4: But it's no coincidence that the major newspapers are owned by Jews and him being charged with a hate crime. They should be charged. They're the ones who keep printing what he said over and over again. They pressured the government to lay those charges.

JASMINE: Oh my god, it's a conspiracy! You livin' in a tinfoil tipi or something? New caller, you're on.

CALLER 3: Boycott Israel!

JASMINE: Ah shit, I thought I cut her off. Must've hit the wrong button. OK, new caller, what's on your mind?

CALLER 5: Dr. Winter is a great man. If it wasn't for him we wouldn't have our own university. We wouldn't have our rights guaranteed in the constitution. He stood up to the government when they tried to wipe away the treaties. And he was firing us up to stand up for ourselves. That's why the government is charging him! To silence him and keep us on our knees.

JASMINE: Good to remember these things about him. Has what he said diminished those accomplishments?

Scene 7

Crash site. The blizzard still rages. A small shelter of pine boughs. DOUG lies in it, shaking despite the small fire that burns in front of him. GORDON returns with some fire wood and a sleeping bag.

GORDON: I can't find your first aid kit. But I found this.

He lays the sleeping bag down and builds up the fire.

You'll be warmer in this.

DOUG: If I die, my family will get fifteen thousand in insurance.

GORDON: I'm sure they'd rather have you than money.

DOUG: I can't feel my legs, Gord. A cripple can't fly. That's all I know. They can start again with the money.

GORDON: Stop talking like that.

DOUG: You should've let him shoot me.

GORDON: You didn't seem too keen on the idea when he was pointing the gun at you. All right, let's get you into this. *(Opens the sleeping bag.)* Ready?

DOUG: No.

GORDON: Neither am I.

He quickly rolls DOUG into the sleeping bag. DOUG screams. GORDON quickly strips off his clothes and hops in next to him.

DOUG: What are you doing?

GORDON: Keeping you from freezing to death.

He undresses DOUG and presses his body against his.

DOUG: Where's Isiah?

GORDON: He took off. We'll get him later.

DOUG: What was he charged with anyway?

GORDON: Public drunkenness.

DOUG: And?

GORDON: That's it.

DOUG: Being a drunk? I crashed my fucking plane picking up a fucking drunk? Christ! I'm still paying off that plane. You couldn't just fine him and let him go?

GORDON: Not my call.

DOUG: Isiah said we should've stayed in Pelican. Bad storm coming. I knew in my gut he was right. I've been flying up here long enough to know that those old guys are always right about shit like that. But the weather office said all clear and I wanted to get back home for Nadia's birthday party. "All clear" my ass. I should've listened to him.

GORDON: Stop wasting your energy.

DOUG: I won't see my kids again.

GORDON: Goddamn right you're going to see them again.

DOUG stops shaking.

DOUG: You believe in God, Gordon?

GORDON: Only when the priest was strapping me.

DOUG: I didn't. Until I started flying up here. The first time I flew north, past La Ronge, I cried. It was so beautiful. I started bawling. Honest. I'm not afraid to admit it anymore. From 10,000 feet up—the sun burning red in the morning—catching the fog on top of them pines—I felt like I was witnessing the first day of Creation. Endless, Gordon, it's fucking endless. Nothing but forest and freedom from horizon to horizon. If I die here…

GORDON: You're not dying here.

DOUG: Then I know it'll be in God's embrace.

DOUG falls asleep.

GORDON: Doug, wake up. You got to stay awake.

ISIAH enters with a couple of dead muskrats.

ISIAH: Well if I knew it was going to be a party I would've brought some beer. *(Laughs.)* So you like being in bed with the white man, eh? Those Anglicans trained you well.

GORDON: Go to hell.

ISIAH: I'm sure I will. Did they call you sinner while they fingered your asshole? Scream "God forgive us our trespasses!" with both hands around your face, their thumbs pressed into your cheeks so you won't bite down. Eyes rolled back until only the whites were showing, lips peeled back, and making that sucking sucking sucking sound through their teeth—hissing "Oh Lord, Who art in Heaven, Hallowed be thy Name, Thy Kingdom come, Thy will be done, on Earth as it is in Heaven!" They're going to heaven. They keep saying so. Must know—it's their god. Powerful that god. He gives them that prayer that drains our spirit—drains our power. It's bad medicine. And it's working. "As we forgive those who trespass against us?" They've been trespassing here for years and we keep forgiving them! They're nothing but famished ghosts—there's not enough for them to eat—their thirst never ends—they never stop shitting and pissing on us because they know we will forgive them. And we do. Again and again. Because of that prayer. You want that kind of salvation, Red Coat? Leave him. Saving his skin won't save yours. *(Pause.)* Fine then. *(Drops the muskrats.)* Muskrat. They're still fat. Caught them sleeping. Remember, these ghosts have just one way to say "thank you" to the Indian.

ISIAH exits humming "Soldiers of Christ, Arise."

Scene 8

The trial. The courtroom. The STENOGRAPHER is preparing the room, making sure water jugs are filled, notepads are evenly laid out, pencils are sharpened and the portrait of Queen Elizabeth hangs just right. A lone REPORTER waits near the entrance. A protester, with a sign that reads "Free Palestein!"—yes, it is purposely misspelled—tap dances, badly around the courtroom, annoying the reporter.

PROTESTER: Stop the Palestinian genocide! Boycott Israel! Stop the Palestinian genocide! Boycott Israel!

GORDON enters. The REPORTER and PROTESTER pounce, speaking at the same time.

REPORTER: Why won't you apologize? How do you feel about the national chief condemning your statements? Do you believe Jews started the Second World War? The Two-Spirited Alliance has said you no longer represent true First Nations values, what do you say about that?

PROTESTER: Stop the Palestinian genocide! Boycott Israel! Stop the Palestinian genocide! Boycott Israel! Stop the Palestinian genocide! Boycott Israel! Stop the Palestinian genocide! Boycott Israel! Stop the Palestinian genocide! Boycott Israel! Stop the Palestinian genocide! Boycott Israel!

GORDON ignores them both and enters the courtroom and the REPORTER and PROTESTER stop. FRANK enters. The REPORTER scrums him. The PROTESTER tap dances around them, trying to get the sign into the shot.

REPORTER: It's been over a year since the Crown filed charges, do you think you can still get a conviction?

FRANK: We're happy to finally get to trial and think that, at the end of the day, justice will be served even if it has been a year.

PROTESTER: *(Into camera.)* Stop the Palestinian genocide! Boycott Israel!

FRANK then escapes into the safety of the courtroom. He paces in the courtroom, practicing his opening argument. The REPORTER glares at the PROTESTER.

REPORTER: I'm trying to do a job here, all right. You've made your point. Now get out of here. Hit the road. Piss off. This is serious business.

PROTESTER: Boycott Israel!

CYNTHIA enters and freezes when she sees the REPORTER. Everyone stands ready, the REPORTER with his questions, the PROTESTER with her sign. The REPORTER shoots her warning looks. A weird kind of fake out game is played by the REPORTER and the PROTESTER. CYNTHIA shrieks and runs into the court making the REPORTER and PROTESTER collide.

REPORTER: Goddamn it!

Stomps away.

PROTESTER: Boycott…Israel…

Alone, she sulks away. The Hon. CARL SMITH, the judge, arrives.

STENOGRAPHER: All rise! The Honourable Carl Smith presiding.

The judge sits. The STENOGRAPHER pours him a glass of water.

CARL: Thank you, dear. *(To CYNTHIA.)* I trust I'm "Gentile" enough for you, Miss Henhawk.

CYNTHIA: Well, your honour, that really wasn't— [the point.]

CARL: Then let's get this show on the road.

GORDON: Judge, I wish to say something.

CARL: What is it, Mr. Winter?

CYNTHIA: Uh, that's Dr. Winter, your honour.

CARL: So they let you keep that one, eh. What can I do for you, "Dr." Winter?

GORDON: I will represent myself, judge. I don't need this kid sitting next to me.

CARL: That "kid" has been protecting your rights better than you have, Dr. Winter. I won't have this case overturned on appeal because of inadequate counsel for the defense.

FRANK: Whoa, judge, he's not guilty yet. I don't want this appealed either because you got ahead of yourself.

CARL: You'll get your chance to strut before the cameras, Frank. *(To GORDON.)* Sit down, sir. You're stuck with the kid till this is over.

GORDON: I'm not finished, judge.

CARL: Yes, you are, sir. Sit down. *(To FRANK.)* Frank, you're up. Make it quick. I got tickets to the Riders game and I don't want to miss the kick off.

FRANK pulls out a life-size cutout of a Jewish death camp inmate.

FRANK: Basically, judge, the defendant said this was a good idea.

CARL: Nice. Guilty!

CYNTHIA: Ah, your honour—I —we —we haven't had our turn yet?

GORDON: What's the point? They've already got their minds made up.

CARL: Exactly. Guilty.

FRANK: Swish! Nothing but net!

CYNTHIA: Your honour!

CARL: This better be about sentencing or I'm holding you in contempt.

CYNTHIA: I'll be in contempt if I don't say anything. Judge Friedman charged me with protecting Dr. Winter's rights.

CARL signals for her to get on with it.

Your honour, the code says that Dr. Winter must've incited hatred. In order for him to do that, there must be a measure of how much hate he incited. The Crown has not proved that my client incited anything. The only reaction to Dr. Winter's comments have been nothing but universal condemnation of him.

SHALINI in their apartment.

SHALINI: As it should be.

CYNTHIA: They were just words, Shalini.

SHALINI: No, this isn't "sticks and stones." These words were meant to harm, meant to instigate.

CYNTHIA: It doesn't matter if they were meant to harm. The question is did they actually cause any harm? You're always telling me about the troubles your clients have getting apartments and jobs because of their skin colour or accents. You even keep numbers on these incidents, right? *(SHALINI nods.)* I'm going to need them.

SHALINI: You're fucking kidding me. I'm not helping you defend that creep.

CYNTHIA: Please, Shalini. I'm bound by professional standards to defend him to the best of my ability. I need those stats to do that.

SHALINI: You're not getting them.

CYNTHIA: Listen. This is all I'm asking, OK? Just those numbers. Nothing more. Winter and I part ways once the judge makes his decision.

Pause.

SHALINI: You promise?

CYNTHIA: I promise.

CYNTHIA hands her a summons. SHALINI hands her the numbers. Back in court.

CARL: Young lady, the section says "likely lead," the Crown does not have to prove that it will.

CYNTHIA: Then I'd like a ruling on the definition of "likely," your honour. Particularly on how long we can hold "likely" over my client's head? *(She holds up the numbers.)* Because I have certifiable data that proves there have been no increases in any incidents against homosexuals, new immigrants or Jews in Saskatoon since he said those words, over a year ago. No harm, no foul, your honour.

CARL snaps his fingers at the STENOGRAPHER

to retrieve the numbers from CYNTHIA. He glances through them.

CARL: You wish to say anything, Frank?

FRANK: We're good, judge.

CARL: You sure you don't want to confront this evidence? Challenge this data?

FRANK: Should I?

CARL: She's got your ass in a sling, Frank! Do something about it!

FRANK snaps to attention.

FRANK: The Crown calls…

CARL: …the author…

FRANK: The author of this data to the stand.

The STENOGRAPHER escorts SHALINI to the witness stand.

SHALINI: Cynthia?

CYNTHIA: Sorry.

CARL: Oh geeze. I don't suppose you'll swear on the Bible, eh?

SHALINI: What's that supposed to mean?

CARL: Never mind. Make it quick, Frank. Kick off's in a couple of hours and I still gotta drive to Regina.

FRANK: I'm on it, judge. I'm on it. *(To SHALINI.)* Could you please tell us your name.

SHALINI: Shalini O'Malley.

FRANK: O'Malley? Really?

SHALINI: Yes, really.

FRANK: Shalini. That's a pretty name. Where are you from?

SHALINI: Regina.

FRANK: No, I mean, where are you "originally" from?

SHALINI: I was born in Regina.

FRANK: Oh, I see. Where were your parents born?

SHALINI: My mother was born in Vancouver, my dad, Goose Bay.

FRANK: Newfoundland?

SHALINI: Labrador.

FRANK: Which is in Newfoundland.

SHALINI: No, it's in Labrador. You've got a lot to learn about this country.

CARL: Get on with it, Frank.

FRANK: And how is it you have this data?

SHALINI: I work with new immigrants. I help them integrate into Canadian society. Find jobs, housing, learn English. And part of that is tracking how often they face incidents of racial profiling or harassment. Such as when they're denied housing or employment.

FRANK: And you're trying to tell us these incidents have not increased since Dr. Winter's comments were published in the newspaper?

SHALINI: They haven't.

FRANK: Not even a little?

SHALINI: No.

FRANK: A smidge?

SHALINI: It's about the same.

FRANK: Oh. *(Pause.)* You're positive?

CYNTHIA: She's proved the point, your honour.

SHALINI and CYNTHIA alone.

SHALINI: Oh my god oh my god oh my god, he's going to get off because of me, isn't he!

CYNTHIA: I didn't know he would call you to testify.

SHALINI: Cynthia, most of my clients are refugees and they need to trust me. That trust is now being pissed away because they're going to think I agree with Winter! My grandparents fled to Canada so they wouldn't have to live in the constant fear that they'd be murdered by their neighbours. Murders that started with words.

GORDON: What kind of country are we leaving them—

SHALINI: I know, I know! "Filth." He called me "filth," Cynthia. That Hitler had a good plan for people like me.

GORDON: Dirty Injun Dirty Injun!

SHALINI: *(To GORDON.)* Shut the fuck up! What mark would I have to wear in your world? *(She takes the Star of David from the death camp cut out and puts it on her own chest.)* This? Not very original, I know, but why fix it, if it ain't broke.

CYNTHIA: You're not Jewish.

SHALINI: I'm not a "Paki" or a "fag" either. This is his solution to playground taunting. He flipped out because some kids who didn't know any better teased his grandson.

CYNTHIA: He flipped out because his life's work was being attacked by the federal government.

SHALINI: And how does invoking Hitler help that?

CYNTHIA: He only said it once, Shalini. Once.

Back in court.

CARL: Move along, Frank.

FRANK: Certainly, judge. *(To SHALINI.)* Would you say you're familiar with the immigrant experience?

SHALINI: I'm familiar with being brown in a mostly white country.

FRANK: Is that a "yes?"

SHALINI: No. When you're white and from another country, people think you have a cool accent. People tell me to go back to where I came from.

Pause.

FRANK: Oh… I see… Regina…right?

CARL puts on watermelon helmet and waves the tickets.

CARL: For Christ's sakes, Frank, do you have any idea what it took to get these! Green is the colour! Football is the game! Now wrap up so we can all get the hell out of here.

FRANK: Yes, judge. *(To SHALINI.)* Do you think he's guilty?

CYNTHIA: Objection, your honour!

SHALINI: Definitely.

CARL: Good enough for me. *(Points to GORDON.)* Guilty.

The Riders blow a play on TV and everyone groans.

Scene 9

The bar after the verdict. The game is still on. CYNTHIA waves at SHALINI, who just gives her the stink eye. CYNTHIA grabs a drink and sits down. GORDON enters and sits next to CYNTHIA. SHALINI glares at CYNTHIA, then walks out.

GORDON: Losing sucks, don't it. Especially when you know you were right.

He sniffs her drink and recoils.

CYNTHIA: I remember when I first heard about you. University. Contemporary Canadian history. There was a photo of you, in a headdress, staring down Pierre Elliot Trudeau.

GORDON: Yeah, I pissed him off. A lot. But he was pretty tough. For a fairy.

CYNTHIA: I asked my dad about those days. He said you pissed him off a lot too.

GORDON: I didn't take kindly to those blue-eyed "full blooded" Mohawks trying to educate me about my history. Lots of Jew blood in them Mohawks.

CYNTHIA: Jew blood?

GORDON: The only Indians you see with curly hair are on Six Nations. Wonder why that is?

CYNTHIA: Yeah. That's what my dad said. You were a racist back then too. Kept calling Mohawks "the Lost Tribe."

GORDON: *(Laughs.)* Yeah, that used to get them all riled up. Bunch of useless tits. Most of them were shell-shocked from the Vietnam War. What was I supposed to do with "leaders" who kept screaming "Gooks in the wire! Gooks in the wire!" every time they had a nightmare. We were only able to unify because Trudeau was such a conniving prick. *(Pause.)* You did good in there. Smart move, getting those stats.

CYNTHIA: She's a friend.

GORDON: That Paki?

CYNTHIA: Good luck, Dr. Winter.

GORDON: Work's not done, Miss Henhawk.

CYNTHIA: Despite my best efforts, the court found you guilty. The case is done, so I'm done.

GORDON: Nothing is done until I say it's done.

CYNTHIA: Who are you to boss me around? The first time we met, you told me to "fuck off." Well now I'm fucking off. You got your wish.

GORDON: We have to appeal.

CYNTHIA: The only thing I have to do is prepare arguments for your sentencing.

GORDON: This wasn't a court, it was a circus. And you know I'm innocent. Or were you just spewing bullshit?

CYNTHIA: It wasn't…bullshit.

GORDON: I'm old, Miss Henhawk. Too fucking old to be kicking ass but what choice do I have? I thought things had gotten better but they haven't. Harper, Martin, Chretien, Mulroney, Turner, Clark, Trudeau—sons of immigrant cocksuckers, all of them! Coming here, ripping off Indian people. Same old story, over and over again.

CYNTHIA: You forgot Kim Campbell.

GORDON: Kim Campbell? Who the hell remembers Kim Campbell?

CYNTHIA: She was our first female prime minister!

GORDON: She wasn't elected.

CYNTHIA: Neither was Turner, you sexist son-of-a-bitch.

Pause. GORDON laughs.

GORDON: You were pretty good in there. Better than that crown prosecutor. But you lost. What happens in there, happens to us out here everyday. Little by little, who we are, what we are gets chipped away. And if we stand up to it and put our hands on the hammers, we get called radical, or terrorist, or criminal. Of course, you can go back to your law practice—forget about being Indian and read your history in books. Or you can reach back into that bloodline of strong Mohawk women I keep hearing about and do something about it.

CYNTHIA: Wouldn't be such a good idea. We didn't like Crees much back then.

GORDON: So what's it going to be?

Pause.

End of Act I.

Act II

Scene 1

We see an actor transform into an old Cree man—she becomes MUSHOM, GORDON's grandfather, and is identified as such. The actor playing GORDON transforms into his six-year old self. We are now at a fish camp, north central Saskatchewan, 1944. GORDON and his MUSHOM are tending a small fire and hanging fish filets for smoking. HAUPTMANN KRUPINSKI enters. He looks really ragged. GORDON sees him.

GORDON: Mushom!

KRUPINSKI: Hilfe… Bitte.

KRUPINSKI collapses. MUSHOM runs to KRUPINSKI's side.

MUSHOM: Quickly, boy. Get him some water.

MUSHOM looks him over carefully. GORDON gets water and brings it to MUSHOM.

Don't worry. He's not going to bite.

GORDON: He talks funny.

MUSHOM: He's a German soldier. *(To KRUPINSKI.)* Wasser. Trinken Sie. Wasser.

He sprinkles the water onto KRUPINSKI's face. It revives him.

Wasser. Trinken.

KRUPINSKI: Wasser…

He's becomes more conscious and gulps the water.

MUSHOM: Easy, easy. Don't get sick.

KRUPINSKI: Danke.

MUSHOM: Bitte.

KRUPINSKI: Sprechen Sie Deutsches?

MUSHOM: Nein. Just the stuff that sounds like English.

KRUPINSKI: Ich habe Hunger. Haben Sie etwas zu essen?

MUSHOM: Hungry?

KRUPINSKi: Ja… Hunger… Essen.

He motions with his hand to his mouth, indicating he wants something to eat.

MUSHOM: Essen! Eat. Yes. *(To GORDON.)* Cut a bunch of small pieces of bannock and bring them to me.

GORDON does what he's told.

GORDON: How can you understand him, Mushom?

MUSHOM: When I was in Europe in the last war, boy. The Germans who surrendered were all starving. Bones with skin hanging off them. All chanting, "Essen, wasser, essen, wasser." Poor buggers were living off rats.

GORDON returns with the bannock. MUSHOM takes a piece and gives it to KRUPINSKI. He devours it.

Slowly. You'll get sick if you eat too fast.

KRUPINSKI nods and chews slowly.

KRUPINSKI: Thank you.

MUSHOM: Ah, so now you speak English?

KRUPINSKI: Sorry. I was a little delirious. I have been wandering these woods for days, maybe weeks. I would have died if I did not find you.

GORDON: Where did he come from, Mushom?

KRUPINSKI: He's very curious. Reminds me of my own sons.

MUSHOM: You're a long way from the prison camp.

KRUPINSKI: If you can somehow tell them where I am, I will gladly go back. No wonder they only had one fence.

MUSHOM: There's a phone at the Indian Agent's house back on the reserve.

KRUPINSKI: You are an Indian?

GORDON: We're Cree Indians.

KRUPINSKI: Forgive me. You do not look like the Indians I see in the books back home. You have no feather headdresses or buckskins.

MUSHOM: Buckskins?

KRUPINSKI: For camouflage in the wilderness.

MUSHOM: We're fishing.

MUSHOM and GORDON laugh.

KRUPINSKI: Yes, you are right. How foolish of me. You do not need to sneak up on a fish in the woods.

GORDON: You don't sound like the white men in town.

MUSHOM: He's from far away.

KRUPINSKI: Any news from the war?

MUSHOM: Still on.

GORDON: I like your jacket.

KRUPINSKI: Not good for the winters here. Or even the fall. Meant for the desert. But I still need it. Will my hat do?

He offers his hat to GORDON. He takes it happily.

GORDON: Mushom. Kihew!

KRUPINKSI: What is that? Ki-hay-yoo?

MUSHOM: It's our word for "eagle." My grandson thinks you're an important man to have that on your hat. What is your name, German?

KRUPINKSI: Anton Krupinski. I'm an officer in the Afrika Korps.

MUSHOM: This here is Gordon. He was named after me.

KRUPINSKI clicks his heels and bows to GORDON.

KRUPINKSI: Pleased to meet you, young Gordon.

MUSHOM: Afrika Korps, eh?

KRUPINSKI: I was wounded and captured at Tobruk in '42. I thought the nights in the desert were cold. Not as cold as here! This…Saskatchewan.

MUSHOM: *(Laughing.)* No, no, I guess not.

KRUPINKSI: So much room here. And green. And wild. Amazing.

GORDON: Mushom, what's a desert?

MUSHOM: I've never seen one.

KRUPINSKI: It's a place with lots and lots of sand and is very, very hot.

MUSHOM: Are you feeling better?

KRUPINSKI: Much. Thank you again. You saved my life.

MUSHOM: You still need to rest.

Scene 2

CYNTHIA and SHALINI's apartment. CYNTHIA has legal books strewn about. She hops from one to the other, glancing through them, making notes. SHALINI enters.

SHALINI: How fucking dare you. How fucking dare you! *(Pause.)* Well?

CYNTHIA: What?

SHALINI: That's all you got to say for yourself? You put me through hell, Cynth, and all you can say is "what" when I find out you've been working on his fucking appeal for six months!

CYNTHIA: Sorry.

SHALINI: No no no. It's too late for sorry. I can't go through this again, Cynth. Not again. You promised!

CYNTHIA: I was right, Shalini. I was right and I lost.

SHALINI: He endorsed genocide, Cynthia! Which is pretty fucked up since your people would've also been sent to the gas chambers if the Nazis had their way.

CYNTHIA: He wasn't convicted of mass murder, he was convicted for speaking his mind. And the judge got it wrong. If I wash my hands of Gordon Winter because he's unpopular—

SHALINI: He's a racist.

CYNTHIA: If we charged everyone with racism then the jails would be packed. I have to do this.

SHALINI: How far do you plan on going with this?

CYNTHIA: Until I can't do it anymore.

Scene 3

CYNTHIA on JASMINE's radio show.

JASMINE: Hooolleeee smokes, listeners! Can you believe it? The Saskatchewan court of appeal has set aside Dr. Gordon Winter's conviction. In a unanimous decision, no less. And sitting in the studio with me is the person who made it happen, Cynthia Henhawk—Indian lawyer supreme. Tawow Cynthia.

CYNTHIA: Sorry?

JASMINE: That means "welcome."

CYNTHIA: Oh. Nia-way. Sey-go.

JASMINE: Say what now?

CYNTHIA: Thank you and hi.

JASMINE: In Mohawk! Nice. Good Indian talk there. We should do that more.

CYNTHIA: That's pretty much all I know.

JASMINE: It's a start. Let's see who's on the line, shall we?

CYNTHIA: What? I thought I was only talking— [to you.]

JASMINE: Caller one, you're on.

CALLER 1: Hey, Jasmine, I want to ask Miss Lawyer there what's going on with the case? Is Dr. Winter still guilty?

CYNTHIA: No, the provincial court of appeal set aside the first conviction but the province has refiled the charges.

JASMINE: So you're back in court?

CYNTHIA: Yes, we are. The province isn't letting up on this.

JASMINE: Interesting. Caller two, what's on your mind?

CALLER 2: Why do you Indians whine and bitch when some guy speaks about equality? You just want your special tax-funded rights so you don't have to work for a living like the rest of us—

JASMINE: Caller three, what say thee?

CALLER 3: Boycott Israel!

JASMINE: Hey you! Stop calling my show! Don't make me send my cousins to punch you in the nose. You hear me? I've had enough of you! Caller four, you're live.

CALLER 4: I'm a survivor of the Holocaust. The Nazis killed my parents, my brothers and sisters, nieces and nephews. I want to know why this man, who has fought oppression his entire life, wishes to oppress other people?

JASMINE: That is a good question.

CYNTHIA: I'm defending him from a criminal charge.

JASMINE: OK, fair enough. But why does he believe these things? I grew up on my reserve, I never heard anyone talk like him.

CYNTHIA: Neither did I and I really, honestly don't know.

JASMINE: He never told you?

CYNTHIA: Never.

Scene 4

The fish camp. 1944. GORDON is wearing the Afrika Korps hat. MUSHOM and KRUPINSKI filet some fish.

GRANT: *(O.S.)* Winter!… Winter!

KRUPINSKI: Who's that?

MUSHOM: I'm not sure.

GRANT: *(O.S.)* Winter!

CONSTABLE DELBERT GRANT enters. KRUPINSKI stands and puts his hands on his head.

MUSHOM: What can I do for you, Constable?

GRANT: You have a guest, Winter.

KRUPINSKI: Hauptmann Anton Krupinski. 90th Light Africa Division. 7-3-5-6-2—

GRANT quickly searches KRUPINSKI.

GRANT: Relax. I know who you are. We've been looking for you for two weeks.

KRUPINSKI: How did you know I was here?

GRANT finishes searching KRUPINSKI.

GRANT: I didn't. *(To MUSHOM.)* I'm here for the boy, Winter. It's October. He's supposed to be in school. You can't keep hiding him in the bush.

MUSHOM: He's too young.

GRANT: He's at least five. Probably older. I like you, Winter. But it's the law. We don't have a choice here. *(To GORDON.)* Come on, son. It's time to go to school.

MUSHOM: Look, Constable. If you walked here, then it's at least two hours back to your car. It'll be dark before then. Camp here tonight. We'll go with you in the morning.

GRANT: What about you, Jerry? You want to spend another night in the woods?

KRUPINSKI: They saved my life.

GRANT: Aiding and comforting the enemy, Winter? I could arrest you for that.

MUSHOM: He was starving, Grant. I'd even do the same for you.

GRANT: That's big of you, old man.

MUSHOM: I still have some lines in the river. Gordon, make our guests some tea.

GORDON does what he's told. MUSHOM exits.

GRANT: I don't get it. We treat you guys like kings. I've seen the camp. You eat better than most Canadians. You even have a swimming pool. My hometown doesn't have a swimming pool. So why do want to escape?

KRUPINSKI: Hauptmann Anton Krupinski. 90th Light— [Afrika Division.]

GRANT: Yeah, yeah, name, rank and serial number. This isn't an interrogation. I'm just asking. Friendly-like.

KRUPINSKI: I'm a soldier. You are my enemy.

GRANT: Even with the swimming pool?

KRUPINSKI: This war isn't about swimming pools. And the camp is still a prison.

GRANT: You're living better off than most.

KRUPINSKI: Why are you taking the boy?

GRANT: The law says all Indian children have to be in a school. Some parents resist. We arrest them and take the children. It's for the best. Cigarette?

He offers a smoke to KRUPINSKI, who accepts it.

KRUPINSKI: Danke.

GRANT: They're wild, like these woods. Superstitious. Simple. Child-like.

GORDON returns with the tea, which he gives to the men. He sits around them, listening intently.

GRANT: If we didn't educate them to our ways, then they'd be lost in this modern world.

KRUPINSKI: They're not meant for our world. They don't belong in it. It would be like taking a wolf cub and making it a pet. Ja, it's a beautiful animal but it's not true to itself. Surely this country's large enough to accommodate them and their ways. What you call "simple" I would call "pure." These woods give them everything they need. I was starving. They fed me. The child seems happy. At least, content.

GRANT: They're not supposed to be here. The old man doesn't have a pass. He's lucky his Indian Agent respects him as a veteran of the Great War and let's these infractions by.

KRUPINSKI: A pass?

GRANT: He needs permission to leave his reserve. We can't have these Indians roaming these woods as they please. If you stop watching them for one second they get into all sorts of trouble. These children need proper guidance. *(To GORDON.)* Are you baptized, son?

GORDON: What's baptized?

GRANT: *(To KRUPINKSI.)* See? Probably hasn't seen the inside of a church yet. The government has no choice. It's best to remove them.

KRUPINSKI: That's horrible.

GRANT: We're making them better humans.

KRUPINSKI: But they are inherently noble.

GRANT: *(To GORDON.)* Come here, son. *(He shows GORDON to KRUPINSKI.)* His face is dirty. Probably hasn't had a bath in weeks. His clothes are ragged. He smells. And what have his people accomplished? Their music is primitive. Their language doesn't have an alphabet. This is noble?

KRUPINSKI: Yes, but they are free from the moral corruptions of our world. They are pure. They do not understand the chains that the Zionist-Bolsheviks are waiting to clamp upon them. And I for one would rather they never knew that. We Germans understood that. We rose up against it. And the entire world rose up against us. They think they are doing the right thing but they were tricked by the Jews into fighting us. We may lose this war but at least we were free for a few years.

GRANT: Well you shouldn't have invaded Poland.

KRUSPINKI: Poland? What the hell do you care about Poland? We were reclaiming German land for German people. Land stolen from us. That's all we wanted. Our land.

KRUPINSKI exits.

Scene 5

GRANT takes GORDON's hand and walks him to the residential school. The residential school students march quietly in the background, pinning their braids to a wall as they enter the school. GRANT turns into PRINCIPAL McADAMS. He grabs GORDON by his hair.

McADAMS: Come here, you filthy brat!

He tries to cut GORDON's braids off. GORDON struggles to protect his head. McADAMS grabs the Afrika Korps hat.

What in the name of King George is this! The uniform of the enemy? Canadian boys are dying in France and Italy to destroy this scourge, this savagery! Let go. Let it go, you little heathen!

They fight over the hat. McADAMS wins.

God, you stink. Nothing a good delousing and a shower won't cure. Welcome to God's house, child. Your eternal soul will thank me.

The other CHILDREN kneel in a row, their hands clasped in silent prayer. McADAMS forces GORDON to kneel.

(To the CHILDREN.) Teach him how to pray.

McADAMS exits.

DANIEL: Psst. What's your name, kid?

GORDON: Gordon.

DANIEL: Well, Gordon. I have to teach you how to pray.

GORDON: I know how to pray. Mushom taught me.

DANIEL: You can't pray like that here. You'll go to hell. You don't ever pray like that again.

GORDON: What's hell?

DANIEL: It's where your skin is burned off over and over again.

GORDON: More than once?

DANIEL: Over and over again. For eternity.

GORDON: Eternity? What's that?

DANIEL: For a long long time. Over and over again.

GORDON: Why!

DANIEL: Because you prayed wrong.

GORDON: How am I supposed to pray?

DANIEL: Like this.

DANIEL leans over and whispers into GORDON's ear. McADAMS returns.

McADAMS: Have you learned how to pray, Gordon?

GORDON nods nervously.

Then let's hear it.

Pause.

Come on, child.

GORDON: Though I walk through the valley of the shadow of death, I will fear no evil.

McADAMS: Good. Continue.

GORDON: For I am the biggest, baddest motherfucker in the valley.

McADAMS: What!

The other CHILDREN scream with laughter.

McADAMS removes his belt and beats GORDON viciously.

You dirty Indian! You dirty, dirty Indian!

CHILDREN: *(Chanting, laughing.)* Dirty Injun Dirty Injun Dirty Injun!

McADAMS: Quiet!

Silence. He glares at GORDON.

Children, your hymn books. "Soldiers of Christ, Arise."

The CHILDREN open their hymnals. PRINCIPAL McADAMS wraps the belt around GORDON's neck and forces him to kneel. He pets and strokes GORDON as if he were a dog throughout the singing of the hymn. GORDON cringes. In the background, ISIAH appears, grinning and waving his arms wildly like some crazed choirmaster.

McADAMS
& CHILDREN: *(Singing.)* Soldiers of Christ, arise/And put your armor on,/Strong in the strength which God supplies Through his eternal Son;/Strong in the Lord of Hosts,/And in His mighty pow'r,/Who in the strength of Jesus trusts/Is more than conqueror.

They continue humming the hymn through the following.

ISIAH: He's grooming you.

GORDON: I prayed everyday. I prayed that the Afrika Korps would come and kill everyone of them and burn this place down.

McADAMS: You people are so beautiful. So wild. So seductive. Only the devil would give such savage people so much beauty.

ISIAH: It's a war. And he is the soldier. Your soul is what he fights for.

GORDON: Krupinski will save me!

ISIAH: The Afrika Korps cannot save you.

McADAMS: But the fires of hell do not need to be your birthright. You can shake the devil's curse. You can choose to be free.

ISIAH: Free. You can still be a wolf. Hunted. Feared. Or you can be a dog.

GORDON: I am not a dog!

GORDON stands at attention in his RCMP uniform.

ISIAH: I found your gun, Red Coat.

Hands him a revolver. ISIAH disappears. PRINCIPAL McADAMS removes the leash.

McADAMS: We made a proper man of you. No one will see the Indian now.

Scene 6

The crash scene. DOUG NAPIER is in the sleeping bag. GORDON enters. He's clutching his side. He sits next to the sleeping bag and opens his jacket, it's bloody. He grimaces. DOUG wakes up. GORDON closes his jacket.

GORDON: The snow's stopped.

DOUG: I feel so warm.

GORDON: Found the first aid kit. Shot you with morphine.

DOUG: I can't feel my legs, Gord. That's not because of the morphine. It doesn't paralyze you. I can move my arms.

GORDON: Stay as still as you can.

DOUG: You say that after you ripped me out of the fucking plane! Don't move? If I'm crippled, it's because you crippled me! *(Pause.)* How much morphine is left?

GORDON: Not enough.

DOUG: Just give me all of it.

GORDON: I made some muskrat soup.

DOUG: I'm not hungry.

GORDON takes a small pot of soup and sits next to DOUG. He puts the spoon into the soup and offers it to DOUG. DOUG turns his head.

GORDON: Eat.

DOUG: Fuck off.

GORDON: You need to eat.

He offers the spoonful again. DOUG refuses. GORDON grabs DOUG's face, squeezes his jaw until it opens and forces the spoon into DOUG's mouth. He then holds DOUG's mouth shut, forcing him to swallow. DOUG coughs and sputters.

DOUG: What the fuck! Get the fuck away from me, asshole!

GORDON: You're going to eat.

He offers another spoonful. DOUG opens his mouth. GORDON feeds him. He alternates giving DOUG soup with himself.

Chew slowly. Muskrats have tiny bones. I think I got them all. But you should eat slow. It'll satisfy the hunger.

He pulls a bone out of his mouth.

Back bone.

He puts it back into his mouth and chews it.

Can't waste nothing. If my Mushom was with us, we'd be eating better, more than a couple of wah-jus-skwak. He was a real bush Indian. This was his home. He taught me some, as much as he could. But the police took me to residential school when I was six.

DOUG: You're bleeding.

GORDON: Not badly.

DOUG: What happened?

GORDON: Got cut up in the crash.

DOUG: It doesn't look good. You okay?

GORDON: I'll make it.

DOUG: You been bleeding all this time?

GORDON: Eat your soup.

DOUG: It's disgusting.

GORDON: Beats starving to death.

DOUG: Not by much. *(Pause.)* Wait! I think I hear a plane.

GORDON: Nice try.

DOUG: I'm serious. Listen. *(Pause.)* An Otter. That's an Otter! I know what that engine sounds like. I'd know it anywhere.

The sounds of an airplane get louder. GORDON stands, grabs a blanket and waves. He's very weak.

GORDON: Hey! Over here!

DOUG waves frantically.

DOUG: We're down here, you bastards! Down here!

GORDON collapses.

Gordon? Gordon!

Scene 7

The REPORTERS enter, one pushing a wheelchair that they place DOUG in. The others lift up GORDON, dust him off, straighten his hat, wipe his face. They then pose GORDON and DOUG together and fire off questions and flash bulbs.

REPORTERS: This way Mr. Napier. Smile Constable. How does it feel to be a hero? Please, Mr. Napier, smile a little. Hold his hand up Constable. Would you call this a miracle? What happened to the prisoner? This way Constable. How do you feel about Constable Gordon saving your life? Did you eat the prisoner to stay alive? Did you pray? Stand a little closer together please. Do you have something to say to your families? Mr. Napier why did you fly into the blizzard?

That stops everyone cold. DOUG blinks uncomfortably into the lights. Silence. The REPORTERS lean closer in, waiting for an answer.

DOUG: Uhhhh…the weather office— [said all clear.]

REPORTERS: Constable Gordon, we have a phone in the other room, the Premier of Saskatchewan wants to congratulate you, personally. Constable Gordon, how do you feel about receiving the medal of bravery. Do you feel honoured to be presented this award from the Queen, herself?

QUEEN ELIZABETH II enters and pins a medal on GORDON. The REPORTERS hum "God Save the Queen." They freeze in that position as flashes hit them from all angles.

Scene 8

The apartment. SHALINI packs her things. CYNTHIA enters.

CYNTHIA: You're leaving?

SHALINI: Just don't say anything, OK. It'll be easier.

CYNTHIA: We can't break the lease, we still have— [six more months.]

SHALINI: I don't care about the lease! Jesus.

CYNTHIA: So you're just going to run?

SHALINI: I advise women all the time to leave when they're in a no-win situation. Find a safe place, then figure shit out.

CYNTHIA: Are you calling me an abuser?

SHALINI: Yes! Yes, I am. I don't feel safe here. In my own home. Knowing that you're working for him. I could forgive it the first time because you were ordered by a judge. But now?

CYNTHIA: Don't you think you're overreacting?

SHALINI: Better safe than sorry.

CYNTHIA: I would never hurt you, on purpose.

SHALINI: You blind-sided me at the trial.

CYNTHIA: It was Tkachuk who called you to the stand.

SHALINI: Because I gave you those numbers! And you didn't stop him.

CYNTHIA: I couldn't. The judge said he had the right to confront the evidence.

SHALINI: Then you should have told me what I was getting into. I can't trust you now.

CYNTHIA: I'm sorry, Shal. I should've seen it coming. I'm sorry.

SHALINI: No. You're too good to be caught off guard like that.

CYNTHIA: I didn't lie to you.

SHALINI: I want to believe you didn't. And it doesn't matter if you did. Not anymore. You got what you needed and that was all that mattered to you. You're different now. It's like his sickness has infected you. You don't care how you get what you need. I'll be back in an hour for the rest of my stuff. Don't be here.

SHALINI storms away.

Scene 9

DOUG, wheels around aimlessly, then starts ramming his wheelchair into a door stop. GORDON enters.

GORDON: Buddy, calm down.

DOUG: Go to hell, Indian!

GORDON: Doug?

DOUG: Who's asking?

GORDON: It's Gordon.

DOUG: Gordon Gordon Gordon, fuck, it's Gordon. Hip hip fucking hooray, it's the great hero, Gordon Winter. I'm so fucking happy to see you, fucker. You here to save me again? Here to tell the world how you carried my ass for three days while you nearly bled to death? Huh? How I didn't know what the fuck I was doing because I took off in a blizzard.

GORDON I never blamed you for the crash.

DOUG: You didn't fucking have to! They did! Those goddamn reporters blamed me, Gordon. They fucking blamed me for the crash and made you some fucking hero. You get a fucking medal from the fucking Queen and I get a tube stuck up my ass to clean out my bowels! Is that fair, Gordon? If I hadn't put down, the way I put down, we all would've died out there but I put down as soft as I fucking could in that fucking blizzard! There ain't a pilot in the world who could've done what I did, but I'm not the fucking hero, you are!

GORDON: Jesus man, you're drunk.

DOUG: You gonna charge me with being crippled under the influence?

GORDON: Calm down. I'm just— [trying to help.]

DOUG: I just want a drink. Just one more drink. In peace. That's my right as a Canadian. To drink in peace without being hassled. I wasn't harming anyone, I just needed to take a piss but I couldn't get into the fucking washroom. I just wanted to go to the fucking washroom but I couldn't get through the fucking doors, Gordon! Not in a wheelchair. I can't take a piss because I am in a wheelchair, Gordon. This fucking wheelchair! Cripples ain't got no rights in this country.

GORDON: Let me take you home. Get cleaned up.

DOUG rams his wheelchair some more against the door.

DOUG: Let me in, motherfuckers! I just want one more drink! Just one more fucking drink!

GORDON: OK, I'm taking you to the station.

DOUG: Jail? You're taking me to jail? I'm already in prison, officer. On this sidewalk. There's no way off it. Not without rolling off a ledge into traffic. If no one wants to help me lift this chair, I'm stuck on the road. It's funny to a lot of people. Watching the cripple pushing his chair against the ledge. And they laugh, Gordon. Fuck they laugh. Hahahahahahaha, look at that piece of shit cripple flop around in his wheelchair. Let's give him a push, eh. Let's give him a push down the fucking road. Down a fucking hill. Yeah, that'll be a fucking hoot!

ISIAH and the REPORTERS enter.

ISIAH: I told you. They can't say thank you.

DOUG: Enough small talk. Gordon Winter, you stand accused of sticking your nose where it don't belong.

GORDON: Because I saved your life?

DOUG: Is that a guilty plea? *(To ISIAH.)* Judge, for your consideration, this man here turned me into this.

ISIAH: What evidence do you have?

ISIAH pulls out the sleeping bag and waves it in GORDON's face.

DOUG: Does this look familiar?

ISIAH: The scene of the crime!

DOUG: I begged you to stop.

GORDON: You would've died.

ISIAH pulls GORDON's gun from his holster.

ISIAH: Found your gun, Red Coat.

DOUG: I'm a pilot. That's all I know.

REPORTERS: A cripple can't fly.

DOUG: Our Father, Who art in Heaven.

GORDON: Don't.

ISIAH gives the gun to DOUG. The REPORTERS approach GORDON with their mics pointed at him. DOUG and the REPORTERS speak at the same time.

DOUG: *(To GORDON.)* The insurance money would've taken care of my family. Instead they had to take care of a fucking cripple. My sons had to see my wife change my diaper because I couldn't take a proper shit on a toilet like a real man. She left me because of that.

Pause.

For Thine is the Kingdom! The power and the glory!

REPORTERS: *(Softly.)* Hallowed be thy Name? Thy Kingdom come? Thy Will be done? On Earth as it is in Heaven? Give us this day our daily bread? And forgive us our trespasses? As we forgive those who trespass against us? Lead us not into temptation? And deliver us from evil?

Pause.

For Thine is the Kingdom. The power and glory.

GORDON: You're blaming me for all this.

DOUG puts the gun under his chin.

DOUG & ISIAH
& REPORTERS: Forever and ever.

GORDON: Don't do this.

GORDON moves towards DOUG but the REPORTERS block him.

DOUG: Amen.

DOUG shoots himself. GORDON collapses, weeping, into ISIAH.

GORDON: No, God, no.

ISIAH: You're welcome, Red Coat.

Scene 10

The bar. GORDON staggers to a table and drops his medal onto it. He orders a beer. KRUPINSKI, much older now, enters. He asks the bar partons some questions, one of them finally points to GORDON. KRUPINSKI walks over.

KRUPINSKI: Excuse me, Constable Winter?

GORDON: I haven't been called Constable Winter for some time. Who's asking?

KRUPINSKI: My name is Anton Krupinski.

GORDON: Krupinksi?

KRUPINSKI: Yes. I was a German prisoner of war. Your grandfather saved my life.

GORDON: That's right! Krupinski! *(Laughs, grasps his hand.)* What are you doing in Canada?

KRUPINKSI: I immigrated. Strange how history works. If it wasn't for the war, I wouldn't have discovered the beauty of this country. And the Canadians were so kind to me when I was a prisoner, well…I didn't want to go back to Germany when the war was over. After I was repatriated, I did everything I could to return. *(Pause.)* I wanted to thank you.

GORDON: Me?

KRUPINKSI: I wouldn't be here if it wasn't for you and your grandfather. Your mushom, I think you called him. Tell me, is he still alive?

GORDON: No. He died when I was in the school.

KRUPINSKI: I'm sorry to hear that.

GORDON: I'm glad you found me. I wanted to thank you, too.

KRUPINSKI: For what, my boy?

GORDON: For the kindness you showed me.

KRUPINKSI: Kindness?

GORDON: You gave me a hat. Eagle with a broken cross under it.

KRUPINKSI: My regimental cap. Yes. Now I remember.

GORDON: Those damn Anglicans took it away when I was sent to the school.

KRUPINKSI: I imagine they did. We were the enemy then. It's amazing how different our world is nowadays. Thirty years ago I was a German prisoner of war and now I am a Canadian citizen. And now you're an RCMP officer. A constable, like Grant was.

GORDON: I'm not a constable anymore. Not after Doug shot himself with my gun.

KRUPINKSI: Yes, I read about it in the newspapers. Very unfortunate.

GORDON: I keep playing it out, over and over again. Trying to see how he got my gun.

KRUPINKSI: Does it matter?

GORDON: Of course it matters! I was disarmed by a drunk cripple.

KRUPINKSI: You were disarmed because of your compassion. And your compassion shames you into thinking it's your fault. Is this why you're here in this place? Staring at your medal wondering if it was worth it? His suicide doesn't change what you did. He had a chance at a new life. He chose not to take it. It is a tragedy, yes. But don't let his suicide destroy you as well. Your people need you.

GORDON: What do you mean by that?

KRUPINSKI: It's a shame how we treat your people. We come here. Newcomers. To this beautiful land. It seems unending, hopeful, open. Your people welcome us and how do we repay that kindness? We come here and take it as our own. And we will keep taking until there is nothing left of you here. Until you have disappeared. Unless you stop it. You don't want to end up like us Germans do you? After what the Jews did in Germany. Nothing was ours anymore. Nothing was German! They kept us in debt to their banks. They worked us to death in their factories. We were on German soil and yet Germans owned nothing. We were only trying to retake what was rightfully ours. We had no choice! *(Pause.)* They too were newcomers once. We showed them kindness. We ignored history. Why do you think Jews have been kicked out of every country they've ever lived in since the time of the Pharoahs? Because they move in and take everything! *(Pause.)* Such ideas are not favourable any more. These are different times now. Why do you not wear your braids?

GORDON: I couldn't. Not while I was in the RCMP.

KRUPINKSI: You are not in the RCMP. Maybe it's time you take back what is rightfully yours.

GORDON: Maybe, it is.

Scene 11

GORDON enters holding an Afrika Korps hat.

CYNTHIA: No, no, no. You can't wear that. The press will go berserk.

GORDON: The eagle clutching the broken cross.

CYNTHIA: That's a swastika under the eagle. Great image, that.

GORDON: Did your folks go to a residential school?

CYNTHIA: No.

GORDON: I learned not to scream or cry. I learned to take it quietly. I can take it. The government of Canada can keep whipping me all they fucking want, I can take it! But my grandchildren? After all these years of fighting for our rights, our recognition, I am not letting that bullshit happen to my grandchildren. The bullshit stops. *(He takes out his medal and shows it to CYNTHIA.)* You haven't seen this yet, have you.

CYNTHIA: Only in the photograph with the Queen. If you wore that to court it would make a better impression. You're a hero. They need to know this.

GORDON: I'm an old man. Who's got one more round in him. Maybe two. But the fighting. Never stops. That bell just keeps ringing. We all have our limits, Miss Henhawk.

We see DOUG, in his wheelchair.

You know, it wasn't that long ago we didn't have handicapped parking stalls. Or ramps into buildings. Or special bathrooms. Eventually, we made room. We accomodated them. Now we think nothing of it.

CYNTHIA: Are you saying we shouldn't?

GORDON: No. I'm saying, it didn't happen without a fight. You look in an older building and you have to wonder, how the fuck did a crippled person make it in Canadian society? The answer is, they didn't. No one gave them that dignity, they fought for it. They still fight for it.

We see KRUPINSKI, who snaps to attention and salutes.

This country is big enough for our people. Enough to accomodate us and our rights and our dignity. I hope you answer that bell when I can't.

The REPORTERS enter, camera flashes and TV lights.

Come on, Miss Henhawk. I still got another round or two in me. Let's see what they got.

REPORTERS: *(Over each other.)* Mr. Winter, Mr. Winter. Do you have anything to say now that you've got a new trial? Any comments before the trial. Are you hopeful? What do you think of the chiefs who are going to Israel? The Canadian Jewish Congress is willing to accept an apology, any comments?

Pause. GORDON puts on the hat and the medal.

GORDON: Though I walk through the valley of the shadow of death. I fear no evil. Because I am the biggest. Baddest. Motherfucker. In the valley.

Pause.

Black out.

The End.